AF726089

Mandy Hargun is a practising solicitor specialising in corporate compliance, data protection, AML and contentious matters. Through extensive experience advising companies, and stakeholders in high pressure situations, she has developed a practical understanding of how conflicts of interest arise, evolve, and are often misinterpreted in day-to-day legal practice. This book reflects her focus on bridging the gap between regulatory theory and real-world application. Drawing on lived experience of managing complex client relationships, regulatory scrutiny, and transactional pressures, Mandy provides clear, grounded guidance designed to support solicitors in exercising sound professional judgment in challenging circumstances.

A Practical Guide to Managing Conflicts of Interest in Law Firms

A Practical Guide to Managing Conflicts of Interest in Law Firms

Mandy Hargun

Solicitor

LLB (Hons)

Law Brief Publishing

Published 2026 by Law Brief Publishing, an imprint of Law Brief Publishing Ltd
30 The Parks
Minehead
Somerset
TA24 8BT

www.lawbriefpublishing.com

Paperback: 978-1-918241-31-0

To those who always support me – thank you.

PREFACE

Conflicts of interest are among the most frequently cited, and yet least clearly understood, areas of legal practice. Despite the simplicity of the SRA Code of Conduct, the distinction between different types of conflicts and the circumstances in which a solicitor may or must cease acting are often misunderstood in practice. In particular, the line between what can be managed and what cannot, is frequently blurred, leading to overly cautious withdrawal in some cases and, in others, a failure to recognise when professional duties have genuinely become compromised.

This book was written to address that gap between the rules as written and the realities of how they operate in practice. The aim of this book is not to restate the Code, but to explore how conflicts arise in real situations, particularly in corporate, transactional, and shareholder contexts where relationships are layered and alignment can shift over time. The focus throughout is on professional judgment: identifying the client, testing alignment, and recognising the point at which continued acting is no longer appropriate. If this book assists solicitors in approaching those decisions with greater clarity and confidence, it will have achieved its purpose.

I am grateful to colleagues and peers who have, often through informal discussion, helped shape the thinking behind this work. I also thank my clients; as without them, I would not have had the opportunity to encounter these scenarios or develop the experience to assist others in navigating them. In particular, I am grateful to those working in compliance and risk roles, whose perspectives on governance and documentation have informed many of the approaches discussed in these chapters.

The law and regulatory guidance stated in this book are believed to be correct and up to date as at 1 March 2026.

Mandy Hargun
March 2026

CONTENTS

CHAPTER ONE

THE SRA'S TWO CONFLICTS THAT MATTER AND WHY LAWYERS STILL CONFUSE THEM

The SRA Code of Conduct ("Code") does not treat all "conflicts" as equal. Nor does it prohibit solicitors from acting simply because a dispute may be contentious, or may involve overlapping relationships between directors, shareholders, and or companies. Instead, the Code identifies two distinct and legally different categories of conflict, each governed by different rules, consequences, and thresholds. Despite this, there is an ongoing confusion between these two categories, which often appear particularly in shareholder and director disputes, which frequently leads to misplaced allegations of impropriety and unnecessary escalation.

Those two categories are personal and client conflicts. The distinction is set out in stark terms in the Code itself. Paragraph 6.1 states:

> "*You do not act if there is an own interest conflict or a significant risk of such a conflict.*" Paragraph 6.2 states "*You do not act in relation to a matter or particular aspect of it if you have a conflict of interest or a significant risk of such a conflict in relation to that matter or aspect of it, unless:*
>
> *(a) the clients have a substantially common interest in relation to the matter or the aspect of it, as appropriate; or*
>
> *(b) the clients are competing for the same objective,*

and the following conditions are met:

> *(i)* *all the clients have given informed consent, given or evidenced in writing, to you acting;*
>
> (ii) *where appropriate, you put in place effective safeguards to protect your clients' confidential information; and*
>
> (iii) *you are satisfied it is reasonable for you to act for all the clients."*

It is important to understand the difference between them, because, surprisingly enough, only one of these categories carries an absolute prohibition on acting.

Personal conflicts

A personal conflict, is one that is referred to in the Code as an "own interest conflict", arises where a solicitor's duty to act in a client's best interests conflicts, or carries a significant risk of conflicting, with the solicitor's *own* personal interests. Paragraph 6.1 is uncompromising, this means that where such a conflict exists, the solicitor must not act and this prohibition is absolute. Client consent, or disclosure, or limited retainers cannot cure this problem.

The SRA guidance makes clear that own interest conflicts are concerned with situations such as a solicitor's financial interest in the outcome, close personal or business relationships, employment relationships, or circumstances where the solicitor would be required to advise on or defend their own conduct. These are the types of situations where independent professional judgment is inherently compromised.

This category is important because it is frequently invoked incorrectly. Opposing solicitors frequently suggest that a firm may be "too close" to particular clients, or is under threat of regulatory reporting, or has invested substantial time and cost in a matter. Such circumstances *may* create commercial or reputational pressure, but they do not, without more (as in additional facts), amount to an own interest conflict within the meaning of paragraph 6.1. Nor does acting robustly for clients, or rejecting demands from an opposing firm. It is important to note that the Code is not concerned with reputational discomfort or tactical pressure. In practice, conflict allegations are sometimes raised as part of the wider tactics of a dispute. Letters threatening regulatory complaints or asserting a lack of independence can put real pressure on a firm, particularly in contentious matters. That pressure, however uncomfortable, does not in itself mean the Code has been breached. Solicitors should be careful not to equate the existence of criticism with the existence of a conflict. The correct approach is to analyse the position against the Code and the facts, rather than withdrawing simply because an opponent demands it. Many will recognise this dynamic from experience. The pressure can be real, and the instinct to withdraw in order to eliminate perceived risk is understandable. But professional judgment requires analysis, not reaction. In situations of genuine uncertainty, the best course is to involve the firm's Compliance Officer for Legal Practice ("COLP") at an early stage, document the assessment, and, where appropriate, seek external regulatory or ethics advice. Early escalation is not a sign of weakness and nor is it a blocker, it is simply – good governance. What matters is, that the decision to continue or to withdraw is reasoned, well recorded, and grounded in the Code, and one that is not driven by the tone of an opposing firms' correspondence.

In circumstances of this kind, you must be sure that there is no indication of any personal financial interest beyond ordinary professional fees, no personal relationship capable of impairing independent judgment, and no requirement for the solicitor to advise on or defend their own conduct in a way that would prejudice a client. Where a firm has properly identified potential risks, undertaken internal analysis, and documented its assessment and ongoing monitoring, that is generally inconsistent with paragraph 6.1 being engaged. In such a situation, the absolute prohibition on acting does not arise.

By way of example, consider a situation in which a solicitor is asked to advise a corporate client in relation to a proposed investment transaction, while the solicitor personally holds shares in the opposing company whose valuation is directly affected by the outcome of that transaction. The solicitor's financial interest in the opposing entity creates a clear risk that their professional judgment may be influenced consciously or unconsciously by their personal financial position. In such circumstances, there is a direct conflict between the solicitor's duty under SRA Principle 7 *to act in the best interests of each client* and the solicitor's own financial interests under Paragraph 6.1 of the Code. There is no exception permitting the solicitor to continue to act with informed consent. Nor would disclosure of the shareholding, putting in place information barriers, or limiting the scope of the retainer suffice. This prohibition is absolute. The appropriate course here would be to decline or cease to act. It is important to note, that is some circumstances, if the conflict is genuinely personal to an individual solicitor and can be entirely isolated from the firm's wider interests, another fee earner reassignment may be considered. However, where the financial interest is held by a partner or is otherwise capable of influencing the firm's independence, internal transfer may not cure the conflict.

It is clear that not every form of commercial pressure or reputational concern constitutes an own interest conflict. For instance, a firm's desire to preserve an ongoing client relationship, to avoid adverse publicity, or to resist aggressive correspondence from an opposing firm does not, without more, amount to an own interest conflict. Such matters require careful professional judgment and robust risk management, but they do not inherently compromise independence in the sense contemplated by paragraph 6.1.

The question that needs to be asked is whether the solicitor's personal interests create a *real and significant risk* of divergence from the client's best interests. Where the only interest at stake is the ordinary recovery of professional fees for work properly done, the Code does not treat this as an own interest conflict. The regulatory focus is on the impairment of independence, not ordinary commercial reality.

Client conflicts

Paragraph 6.2 deals with conflicts between clients, often referred to as professional conflicts. This can arise where a solicitor owes duties to two or more clients in the same or a related matter, and those duties conflict, or there is a significant risk that they may conflict. Importantly, paragraph 6.2 does not impose an absolute ban. Instead, it establishes a default rule against acting, subject to defined exceptions and this is important to understand.

Many disputes particularly those involving companies, directors, and shareholders may naturally give rise to a risk of conflict. The SRA does not require firms to avoid all risk; it requires firms to identify, assess, manage, and continuously monitor and review *that* risk.

Consider a situation in which a firm acts for a company and also for certain shareholders and directors in their personal capacities, while an ongoing dispute involves another stakeholder who may not be a client of the firm. That structure plainly gives rise to at least a significant risk of conflict. The firm owes duties to the company as a separate legal entity, and to the individual shareholders or directors personally, and those duties – may not always align. The existence of that risk must be expressly identified and understood from the outset. So the critical question is, not whether a risk exists, clearly it does, but whether the firm can properly rely on one of the exceptions under paragraph 6.2.

The risk becomes more material where, for example, one of the shareholder/directors seeks to secure additional personal financial terms in the course of the dispute that would benefit them individually but would not align with the company's best interests or the interests of the shareholders as a whole. At that stage, alignment can no longer be assumed. The firm must consider whether the substantial common interest continues to exist, or whether the situation has crystallised into an actual client conflict. In this scenario, the solicitor owes separate duties to the company and to the individual shareholder. If the shareholder's personal objective conflicts with the company's interests, those duties will naturally pull in different directions. The starting point under paragraph 6.2 is that the solicitor must not act where there is a conflict of interest or a significant risk of one. The firm may *only* continue to act if it can properly rely on one of the two limited exceptions, namely, that the clients have a substantially common interest, or that they are competing for the same objective. Even then, the firm would need to ensure; all affected clients give informed consent in writing; appropriate safeguards must be implemented where necessary to protect confidential information; and the firm must be satisfied that it *is* reasonable to act for all clients.

If the divergence of interests means that there is no longer a substantially common interest, and the matter does not fall within the "competing for the same objective" exception, the firm cannot continue to act merely because safeguards are in place. Where the exceptions under paragraph 6.2 no longer apply, the firm cannot continue to act for both clients. Whether it may continue to act for one depends on its ongoing duties of confidentiality and loyalty to the other. In some cases, withdrawal from all affected clients may be necessary; in others, it may be possible to continue for one client only, provided that doing so does not involve misuse of confidential information or create unfairness. Such an example illustrates the difference between a manageable risk and a disqualifying conflict. Paragraph 6.2 permits acting only within tightly defined boundaries. Once those boundaries are crossed, continued acting is no longer a matter of discretion.

What does substantial common interest mean?

The first and most relevant exception permits a firm to act where the clients have a substantially common interest in relation to the matter. The SRA guidance explains that this requires more than superficial alignment; there must be a clear shared purpose and a strong consensus on how that purpose is to be achieved.

So, considering our scenario in a different context; where the company and the shareholders/directors were to share such a common interest, and they are aligned, any advice given to the company would be grounded in directors' statutory duties under sections 171 and 172 of the Companies Act 2006 and is consistent with the position advanced by the shareholders/directors in their personal capacities. Even then, this alignment cannot be assumed blindly. It would need to evidenced by board resolutions, correspondence, and consistent instructions. The firm has also taken steps to ensure that the company's instructions are given through a properly constituted board, rather than informally through individuals acting in their own interests.

Under Paragraph 6.2 of the SRA Code of Conduct, solicitors are permitted to act for multiple clients with conflicting interests in specific situations if those clients share a substantially common interest in relation to the matter at hand.

Where careful consideration is required, is where a law firm representing both a company and its shareholders in a dispute involving the alleged misconduct of a former shareholder, this is where careful consideration is required and things can get messy. The company and the shareholders represented by the firm have a common interest, clear that both parties want to defend the company's position in the dispute and preserve the company's governance and operational stability. The dispute centres on allegations made against a former shareholder, but there is a shared understanding that the company's reputation and future operations must be protected during the legal proceedings, whether they lead to court determination or settlement.

It would be clear that clients are aligned not only in their objectives but also in the way it approaches the matter. The board resolutions demonstrate that the company's instructions are being provided through the appropriate corporate governance structures (the board of directors) and not by individual shareholders acting on their personal interests. This process ensures that the firm's actions are consistent with the best interests of the company, rather than any personal agendas. If the interests of the company and the shareholders begin to diverge significantly, such as if one shareholder begins to act in a way that conflicts with the company's best interests, the firm may need to reconsider its position under Paragraph 6.2 and take steps to manage the risk of conflict.

Consider another scenario where a law firm is representing two companies that are considering a joint venture. Both companies have common interests in ensuring the success of the venture, but there may be potential for internal disputes over the specifics of the terms or the governance of the new entity. However, at the strategic level, both companies are aligned on the end goal of creating a profitable partnership and expanding their market presence. For this common interest exception to apply, the companies would need to have a shared purpose, for instance, they may both aim to enter a new market or develop a new product or service. The law firm can act for both companies, provided that the companies are in agreement about the key terms of the joint venture and share a clear vision for achieving success. This alignment might be evidenced by board resolutions or formal letters of intent, which ensure that the companies are not acting on conflicting individual goals but are instead united by a common commercial objective.

It is important to note that the SRA guidance stresses that the common interest between the clients must go beyond a superficial alignment. There must be a clear shared purpose and a strong consensus about how to achieve that purpose. For example, in corporate disputes or mergers, while clients may share high level goals, such as defending the company's interests, and or ensuring a successful merger, the method of achieving these goals must also be clearly aligned.

This exception allows firms to act for multiple clients even where there might otherwise be a risk of conflict. However, the burden is on the solicitor to ensure that the common interest is not only real but substantial. Mere convenience or formal alignment such as a shared objective without clear commitment to the same strategies will not suffice. Therefore, solicitors must be careful to document and continually monitor the level of common interest between clients and to ensure that both parties are not only aligned at the outset but continue to *remain* aligned, throughout the matter.

Consent and safeguards

Reliance on paragraph 6.2 also requires informed consent, evidenced in writing. Here, informed consent would be required from the shareholders, together with clear confirmation that advice given to the company is for the company's benefit alone and not for them personally. This distinction is important and needs to be expressly documented.

The firm would consider confidentiality risks under Paragraphs 6.3[1], 6.4[2] or 6.5[3]. to ensure there is no adverse interest between the company and the shareholders in their personal capacities that engages paragraph 6.5. However, the firm would also need to recognise that if such adversity were to arise, it would need either to implement effective safeguards ensuring no real risk of disclosure of confidential

---

[1] 6.3 – You keep the affairs of current and former *clients* confidential unless disclosure is required or permitted by law or the *client* consents.

[2] 6.4 – Where you are acting for a *client* on a matter, you make the *client* aware of all information material to the matter of which you have knowledge, except when: (a) the disclosure of the information is prohibited by legal restrictions imposed in the interests of national security or the prevention of crime; (b) your *client* gives informed consent, given or evidenced in writing, to the information not being disclosed to them; (c) you have reason to believe that serious physical or mental injury will be caused to your *client* or another if the information is disclosed; or (d) the information is contained in a privileged document that you have knowledge of only because it has been mistakenly disclosed.

[3] 6.5 – You do not act for a *client* in a matter where that *client* has an interest adverse to the interest of another current or former *client* of you or your business or employer, for whom you or your business or employer holds confidential information which is material to that matter, unless: (a) effective measures have been taken which result in there being no real risk of disclosure of the confidential information; or (b) the current or former *client* whose information you or your business or employer holds has given informed consent, given or evidenced in writing, to you acting, including to any measures taken to protect their information.

information, or to obtain express informed consent from the *affected* client.

There are further safeguards that the firm could consider, such as instructing separate counsel for the company and the shareholders, maintaining separate files, and actively monitoring the position. Of course, these steps do not eliminate the risk, but they are relevant to the *reasonableness* assessment required by paragraph 6.2(b)(iii). In obtaining informed consent, it is essential that all parties understand the nature of the conflict and the scope of the firm's role. Engagement letters should clearly set out the terms of representation, including the fact that the solicitor is acting for all parties involved and that the advice provided to the company is for its benefit and not for the personal benefit of the shareholders. The engagement letter should also outline the firm's commitment to adhering to the SRA Code, ensuring that the solicitor will act independently and in compliance with all ethical and regulatory requirements, even in the face of potential conflicts. The firm should also ensure that clients are made aware of their right to seek independent legal advice, providing transparency about the potential risks and ensuring that their consent is truly voluntary and based on a clear understanding of the situation.

Where could the line be crossed?

The answer is not always as clear cut, as such circumstances require careful analysis and continuous monitoring. For example, if the company were required, under its articles of association or statute, to register a shareholder, but a shareholder personally wished to prevent this outcome, the firm could not advise both parties on directly conflicting positions. In such a situation, this would constitute a client conflict under paragraph 6.2. Similarly, if a suspended director were reinstated, such that the board would no longer have the lawful authority to instruct the firm, or if litigation progressed to a point where liability between directors became a live issue, the shared interest between the company and the individual directors would no longer hold. In such cases, continuing to act for both parties may not be permissible under paragraph 6.2. The question of whether it could continue to act for one, would depend on its duties of confidentiality and the reasonableness of doing so. In some circumstances, withdrawal from both may be required, again this would require careful analysis and an independent advisor may be sought for impartial advice.

The firm's recognition of these potential limitations is not a flaw but rather a demonstration of proper compliance with the SRA Code. The Code does not require solicitors to predict the future and foresee every possible conflict in advance. Instead, it demands that solicitors exercise ongoing professional judgment, continuously assessing and managing conflicts of interest as circumstances of each scenario evolves.

Why we can get this wrong

Much of the criticism advanced by opposing firms conflates neutrality with independence, and independence with disengagement. The SRA Code does not require a solicitor acting for a company to act as a referee between shareholders, nor to treat non clients as clients. The solicitor's duty is to act in the best interests of the client it represents, subject to managing conflicts as defined by the Code.

Allegations that a firm cannot act neutral simply because it also acts for aligned shareholders misunderstand both company law and the SRA framework. The relevant question is not whether someone else objects, but whether the solicitor's duties to current clients are incompatible.

For example, in the scenario where a law firm is representing a company and multiple aligned shareholders in a corporate transaction, the firm's duty is to act in the best interests of its clients, namely the company and the shareholders it represents. A shareholder may object to the firm's advice or decisions regarding the transaction, but that objection does not, on its own, create a conflict of interest. The firm's role is not to serve as a neutral party between the shareholders but to ensure that each client receives advice tailored to their specific interests within the framework of the matter at hand.

If, for example, one shareholder disagrees with the proposed sale price of shares, this may not in itself is an inherent conflict unless that shareholder's interests diverge fundamentally from those of the other shareholders or the company, requiring a reassessment of the firm's position under Paragraph 6.2 of the SRA Code. The firm is not required to mediate between shareholders, but rather to continue representing each client within the bounds of professional conduct and without compromising its duty to act in their best interests.

Conclusion

Properly understood, the SRA's conflict rules are both stricter and narrower than is often suggested. Paragraph 6.1 imposes an absolute bar where a solicitor's own interests are engaged. Paragraph 6.2 permits acting in situations of risk, provided the firm can demonstrate substantial common interest, informed consent, appropriate safeguards, and reasonableness.

The real ethical risk lies not in acting where the Code permits it, but in failing to recognise the moment when alignment ends. Where that moment has not yet arrived, it must remain under constant review as part of ongoing risk management. Some factors to consider include:

- Changes in the nature of the clients' relationship, such as if a client begins to pursue interests that diverge from the original alignment, or if a client's goals become incompatible with the overall shared purpose, this could signal that the alignment is ending;

- If, for instance, a legal or factual developments arise that put the clients' positions at odds with one another, such as disputes over the interpretation of key contract terms or a new legal issue that could create an adversarial relationship and this might trigger the need to reassess the conflict;

- If the matter becomes more high-stakes, whether through financial implications, reputational concerns, or regulatory scrutiny, what may have been manageable as a conflict at one stage could become more *pronounced*, requiring the solicitor to reconsider their ability to continue acting;

- If a client's behaviour changes, or they issue instructions that undermine the firm's ability to act impartially, this should be flagged and considered carefully. This includes any attempt to exert undue influence on the firm's legal advice or strategy.

Firms and solicitors should implement regular reviews with the COLP, and maintain open channels of communication with clients to ensure continued alignment. They should also stay vigilant to any developments that may affect the scope of their duty to each client. This ongoing assessment is critical in managing potential conflicts and ensuring compliance with the SRA Code.

CHAPTER TWO

WHY MANAGING CONFLICTS IS HARDER THAN SPOTTING THEM

Once a potential conflict has been identified, the most difficult question is whether it can lawfully and ethically be managed. Chapter 1 explains how the SRA is only concerned with two types of conflict that truly matter, namely personal conflicts under paragraph 6.1, and client conflicts under paragraph 6.2. We now build on that foundation by examining how those conflicts are approached in practice, why some lawyers may often overestimate their ability to "manage" them, and how the SRA's framework draws a distinction between what is capable of mitigation and what is not. The scenario in Chapter 1 provides a useful real world illustration of how easily these categories can blur, and how careful analysis is required to remain compliant.

Personal conflicts – absolute prohibition, and no room for management

The first and most strict category is the personal, or "own interest", conflict under paragraph 6.1 of the Code. This arises where a solicitor's duty to act in the best interests of a client conflicts, or presents a significant risk of conflict, with the solicitor's own interests.

The SRA's position is unforgiving, if an own interest conflict exists, the solicitor must not act. There are no exceptions, no scope for client consent, and no amount of disclosure or safeguards that can legitimise continuing to act. What is often misunderstood is that a personal conflict is not limited to obvious financial interests. It can arise from prior conduct, reputational exposure, personal relationships, or situations where a solicitor may be asked to assess or investigate their own advice or that of colleagues within the same firm. In a corporate context, a disguised own interest conflict can emerge where a firm's ongoing commercial relationship with powerful individual clients creates an incentive, and this can be conscious or unconscious to shape advice given to a corporate client in a way that protects those individuals. If the firm's independence is compromised by fear of losing lucrative instructions, the conflict is personal to the firm and is therefore non consentable. Client conflicts and its narrow exceptions Client conflicts under Paragraph 6.2 are perhaps more familiar and, in some circumstances, manageable.

A client conflict exists where a solicitor owes separate duties to two or more clients whose interests conflict, or where there is a significant risk that they may conflict, in the same or a related matter. The default rule is that the solicitor must not act. However, as mentioned unlike Paragraph 6.1, Paragraph 6.2 contains two tightly defined exceptions, namely that the clients have a substantially common interest, or the clients are competing for the same objective. Even in these cases, the solicitor may only proceed if three collective conditions are met:

- Informed consent from all affected clients,
- Appropriate safeguards to protect confidential information, and
- A positive assessment that it is reasonable for the solicitor to act for all of them.

The concept of a "substantially common interest" is frequently overstated. It is not enough that clients are currently aligned tactically, or that they share a short term objective. The SRA guidance requires a clear common purpose and a strong consensus on how that purpose is to be achieved. Where interests are capable of diverging as the matter develops, the solicitor must continually monitor whether the common interest remains sufficiently robust.

Examples and reasoning

1. Corporate transaction (substantially common interest)

   A law firm is acting for a company and its majority shareholders in a transaction involving the sale of shares to a third party buyer. Both the company and the majority shareholders have a substantially common interest in ensuring the deal proceeds smoothly, but they may have slightly different motivations regarding the terms of the deal, for example, shareholders may prioritize financial gain, while the company may focus on long term stability post sale. However, as long as their common interest in closing the deal is clear and they are in agreement on the major terms, this could meet the substantially common interest exception. The solicitor must ensure that the common interest remains sufficiently clear and that any divergence between the interests of the company and the shareholders is carefully monitored. In this case, the solicitor should seek informed consent from both parties, explaining the risks and ensuring that the company's best interests are fully protected. Safeguards such as separate legal teams or information barriers may also be implemented to prevent any confidentiality breaches.

2. Family business

Consider a family business in which the parents and children are shareholders and wish to restructure the company. In this scenario, the children wish to sell their shares to a third party, while the parents prefer to buy the shares themselves to maintain family control. In this case, the competing for the same objective exception could apply, as both parties are competing for control of the business. Here, the solicitor could potentially represent both sides if certain safeguards are in place. Informed consent from both parties would be necessary, and the solicitor would need to assess whether it is reasonable to continue representing both parties given the potential for conflict. Strong safeguards would be required to protect confidential information, and the solicitor would need to monitor the situation closely as the matter evolves.

3. Contract negotiations

A law firm representing a joint venture between two companies in negotiating a contract. While both companies share the substantially common interest in completing the deal, their goals may diverge on certain terms, for example, one company is seeking stronger payment terms, while the other is prioritizing more favorable delivery timelines. In such a scenario, the solicitor would need to ensure that the common interest remains sufficiently strong to proceed. If the divergence becomes significant, the solicitor may need to withdraw or seek additional informed consent. The solicitor must continually assess whether the parties' common interest remains substantial or whether it is weakening as the matter progresses. The solicitor should establish clear, documented agreement that reflect the clients' mutual consent to continue representation, while also implementing safeguards to manage any risk of conflicts arising from the differing objectives.

Ongoing monitoring

Where interests are capable of diverging as the matter develops, the solicitor must continually monitor whether the common interest remains sufficiently robust. The key takeaway here is that the solicitor's ongoing judgment plays a critical role in determining whether the conditions set out under Paragraph 6.2 are still met, and whether it remains reasonable for the solicitor to act for both clients.

Paragraph 6.2 in practice

The corporate company/shareholder scenario sits squarely within this analytical framework. The firm is acting for the Company and for the shareholders. There is no dispute that there is at least a significant risk of conflict, the shareholders whose personal interests may diverge from the Company's interests. At this stage, the firm's justification for acting rests on the "substantially common interest" exception. The shareholders and the Company are aligned, for now, on a shared objective. That alignment would be evidenced by board resolutions authorising the firm to act, correspondence confirming instructions, and the absence (at present) of any decision by the Company that would be adverse to the shareholders' personal positions.

Crucially, the firm would need to recognise that this alignment is contingent, not permanent. If the Company were required under its articles or the Companies Act to take a position adverse to the shareholders, or if litigation crystallised issues of liability between shareholders/directors, the common interest could disperse overnight.

Additional things to consider

1. Re-assessment of alignment – the firm must continuously monitor the situation for any developments that could lead to a divergence in the interests of the shareholders and the Company. For example, if a decision is made by the Company's board that contradicts the interests of the shareholders, such as a decision about dividend distribution, the sale of Company assets, or key personnel decisions, the firm may need to reassess its ability to represent both the Company and the shareholders without conflict.

2. Legal obligations – section 172 of the Companies Act 2006 requires directors to act in a way that promotes the success of the Company for the benefit of its shareholders as a whole. If any actions or decisions taken by the board, such as appointing or reinstating directors, conflict with the interests of the individual shareholders, the firm may face a legal conflict. It is important for the firm to regularly review whether any decisions taken by the Company's directors could trigger a conflict of interest and ensure that safeguards are in place to address this.

3. Informed consent – the firm should also ensure that the shareholders have explicitly acknowledged and agreed to the potential for conflicts that may arise as the matter progresses, particularly in situations where their personal interests may diverge from those of the Company. This can be documented in engagement letters and or written confirmations. Moreover, the firm should make it clear to the shareholders that their ability to continue with the same legal representation depends on their ongoing alignment with the Company's position.

4. Confidentiality and information barriers – in case the interests of the shareholders and the Company diverge, the firm must implement appropriate safeguards, such as information barriers (walls), to ensure that confidential information is not shared between the parties in a way that would harm either party. This is especially important if the firm must continue acting for both the Company and the shareholders at different stages of the matter.

5. Professional judgment – the firm must exercise professional judgment at each stage of the matter, continually evaluating the potential risks and conflicts that may arise. As the situation evolves, the firm should remain vigilant and prepared to withdraw from representing one or both parties if the conflict becomes unmanageable, in accordance with Paragraph 6.2 of the Code.

Informed consent, safeguards, and reasonableness

Reliance on paragraph 6.2 requires more than asserting alignment. Informed consent must be real, documented, and ongoing. The real question is whether the firm can protect duties of confidence and loyalty if interests diverge. One such concern that opposing solicitors may raise, is that the the same fee earners appear to be involved on both engagements and that this would highlight the need either for structural separation within the firm or, at a minimum, clearly documented limitations on information sharing agreed by all clients.

Finally, the firm must be satisfied that it is reasonable to act. This requires an honest assessment of whether the Company is genuinely giving independent instructions or whether it is effectively controlled by individual shareholders who are also personal clients. If the latter, the risk is not merely in theory, it undermines the firm's ability to demonstrate that it is acting in the Company's best interests rather than favouring one faction of stakeholders.

Perhaps the most important lesson is that conflict management is not one-off. The SRA expects continual monitoring. The decision to diarise regular reviews, retain board minutes and resolutions, and maintain contemporaneous file notes explaining the rationale for continued acting is not defensive paperwork; it is central to compliance and good governance. Equally important is recognising the exit point. If there were no properly constituted board able to give independent instructions, or if litigation required the firm to investigate or pursue claims against its own individual clients as directors, continued acting would no longer be sustainable. At that point, withdrawal would not be optional but necessary.

Management is conditional

In conclusion, personal conflicts cannot be managed at all. Client conflicts can only be managed within the narrow confines of paragraph 6.2, and only for as long as the factual basis for reliance on an exception remains sound. Essentially, attempting to manage a conflict is permissible; persisting once it has crystallised is not.

CHAPTER THREE

ACTING FOR CLIENTS

Acting for multiple parties in the same transaction

Funnily enough, the difficulty with multi-party transactions is not that they begin in conflict, it is that they begin in agreement. In disputes, division is clear. In transactions, division is deferred. Everyone wants the deal to happen and that shared objective creates a level of comfort, however, it also creates blind spots. Most transactional conflicts do not arise because lawyers misunderstand the rules, they arise because lawyers overestimate the stability of early alignment.

Deal unity

At the outset of an investment, restructure or joint venture, the language is cooperative, you hear these common phrases, "we're aligned", "we're all on the same page", or "we just need the paperwork." Those phrases often leads us to assume that the structure of representation is safe simply because the parties are commercially motivated to complete. But – alignment in a transaction is often conditional. You, see, founders may agree in principle to dilution until control provisions are drafted, investors may accept minority status until veto rights are discussed, and or family shareholders may agree on restructuring until valuation mechanics are defined. The divergence often appears first in drafting, not in meetings, and a solicitor acting for more than one party must recognise that the real risk often begins when drafting becomes specific.

High level agreement can conceal complexity, for example, imagine how quickly divergence appears in provisions dealing with, inter alia:

- Appointment and removal of directors;
- Reserved matters;
- Dividends and distributions;
- Exit rights;
- Transfer of shares;
- Leaver provisions;
- Warranties and indemnities.

In many transactions, the first real tension emerges not because the parties dislike one another, but because the drafting reveals what each party is truly protecting, and this is where the solicitor's position becomes delicate. If acting for multiple parties, you are no longer merely implementing an agreed structure, you are navigating competing allocations of risk. It is here where overconfidence in early alignment can become dangerous.

A consistent feature of complex transactions is the private aside, for example, a director may ask, "off the record, how exposed am I under this warranty?", or a shareholder asking, "can we soften this clause without upsetting them?", or an investor asks, "do the founders really intend to stay long term?". Whilst, each conversation may appear commercially routine, it is increasing in risk of divergence. It is important to note, that the risk is not that the solicitor will intentionally misuse information, it is that they will begin to adjust advice in order to preserve overall deal unity. That is where professional judgment can quietly erode.

The Company Is not the founder

Another recurring difficulty in transactional work is the merging of identity between company and controller. In founder led or family businesses, the distinction between the corporate entity and the individuals behind it can feel somewhat synthetic, this is as instructions come from the same people and decisions are taken collectively. While interests are aligned, this works. Again, when drafting begins to affect personal wealth differently from corporate position, the distinction matters.

Where the company's position consistently mirrors the personal preferences of individual clients, a firm should pause and examine whether it is acting for an entity or a faction.

Time pressure distorts risk perception

The most common misjudgment occurs near completion. By that stage you have spent weeks or months on this matter, timetables are fixed, external stakeholders are waiting, and fees are substantial. If a late divergence appears such as an indemnity expansion benefiting one party at the expense of another represented client, the instinct can be to resolve it quickly, the pressure of "we are nearly there", which can rationalise continued acting. The solicitor must confident in realising that the structure of representation no longer reflects the reality of the deal, and then do something about it.

The grey area

Consider a company raising investment where the firm acts for the company and both founders personally. At heads of terms stage, the interests appear aligned, all parties support the investment, the valuation is agreed in principle, and governance structure is broadly accepted. However, as drafting progresses, one founder expresses uncertainty about long term involvement. Later, that founder asks for protective drafting in the event of removal. Shortly before completion, the same founder requests minor amendments enhancing personal exit protection, without drawing particular attention to their effect. When we consider this in isolation, none of these steps automatically require withdrawal. Holistically, founders would often seek clarity around leaver provisions and exit mechanics. However, taken together, the pattern may signal that the founder's personal interests are beginning to diverge from the shared transaction structure that originally justified acting for these multiple clients.

The difficulty is that there is incremental divergence. The founder's focus has shifted from collective value creation to personal risk mitigation. That shift may begin to place the solicitor in a position where advice to the company about investor confidence conflicts with advice to the founder about enhanced personal protection. It is at this point, the firm must analyse whether the substantially common interest exception can still properly apply. The original common interest securing investment and growing the company may still exist at a high level, however, if one founder is now prioritising exit protection in a manner that could weaken the company's governance position or materially affect investor perception, the alignment may no longer be sufficiently robust. The solicitor must ask whether the clients still share a clear common purpose and consensus on how it is to be achieved, or whether the matter has shifted into a situation where the solicitor would need to advance materially different objectives for different clients.

The reasonableness requirement also becomes critical. Even if informed consent was obtained at the outset, consent does not operate indefinitely if the matrix changes. The firm must consider whether it remains reasonable to act for both the company and the founder where drafting now reallocates risk in a way that benefits one at the potential expense of the other. If the solicitor cannot advise the company fully on the implications of enhanced exit protection without undermining the founder's personal position, or vice versa, then the practical ability to maintain undivided loyalty could be considered compromised. This is the kind of grey area where firms misjudge risk, not because they misunderstand the Code, but because the divergence feels manageable. The deal is still progressing, the investor has not objected, and there is no open dispute. Yet the solicitor's role is no longer neutral drafting; it involves shaping provisions that materially alter the balance of risk between represented clients. The Code permits careful management where a genuine common interest remains. The key question is whether the foundation that justified joint representation still genuinely exists.

Role creep

A further subtle risk in multi-party transactions is role creep. This is where over time, the solicitor can become perceived by the clients and sometimes by themselves as the person holding everything together. In complex transactions involving multiple stakeholders, you need someone to manage the flow of documents, smooth tensions, and to keep negotiations moving.

This, in itself, is not problematic, the difficulty arises when the deal begins to feel like a collective project rather than a matter requiring independent legal judgment at every stage, and objectivity can become compromised. A solicitor may begin to downplay emerging divergence between clients because it may seem commercially manageable, and advice may be framed in a way that preserves momentum rather than fully articulating risk. Internal concerns may also be postponed on the basis that the issue can be "worked through" later. Escalation within the firm to the COLP may also be avoided because it feels disproportionate to what still appears to be a functioning and manageable deal. Now – none of this is usually intentional and rarely driven by bad faith. It is just the product of human dynamics within pressured environments. Completion deadlines, client expectations and invested time all contribute to a subtle shift in focus from independence to preservation.

The duty is not to make the transaction succeed, but to ensure that advice remains clear, objective and undivided. Recognising this, and stepping back at that point is a mark of professional judgment, not obstruction.

Acting against former clients

This raises a different kind of professional risk. The issue is no longer divided loyalty between current clients. It is the continuing duty of confidentiality. The difficulty in this area is often psychological rather than technical. For example, a retainer may have ended years earlier. The relationship may have concluded amicably. The fee earners involved may also have moved on. From a commercial perspective, the former client may feel distant. From a regulatory perspective, however, the duty to protect confidential information does not expire with the engagement letter.

The core question is not whether the firm feels neutral. It is whether the firm holds information that could realistically be relevant to the new matter. In practice, this is where firms misjudge the risk. Confidential information is rarely limited to documents. It includes commercial strategies, negotiation tendencies, internal governance dynamics, appetite for litigation, financial pressure points, settlement thresholds and certain corporate vulnerabilities.

When a new instruction is received against a former client, the firm must pause and consider not simply what it remembers consciously, but what it knows structurally. If the new matter overlaps in subject matter, industry context, contractual framework or commercial structure, the risk increases. For example, acting for a competitor in a transaction involving similar assets may raise concerns even if the assets are different. Acting in litigation arising from a contract drafted during the earlier retainer is more serious. Acting against a former director of a company previously advised may expose strategic information about board dynamics that is not publicly available.

The passage of time does not automatically neutralise risk. Information may remain commercially sensitive long after the original matter concludes. Likewise, the fact that a different fee earner is handling the new matter does not eliminate the firm's collective knowledge.

This is where the concept of unfair advantage becomes relevant. The concern is not intentional misuse. It is whether the firm's knowledge could, even unconsciously, shape advice in a way that disadvantages the former client.

Information barriers/walls may assist in certain circumstances, particularly in larger firms where teams are genuinely separated. However, barriers are not a universal solution. If the information held is directly relevant and material to the new dispute or transaction, internal separation may not be enough to remove the risk. At the outset of a new retainer against a former client, firms should identify:

- The scope and duration of the previous engagement;

- The nature of the information obtained;
- Whether that information remains confidential and commercially sensitive;
- Whether it could realistically be relevant to the new matter.

This assessment should be recorded. If there is any uncertainty, then escalation to the COLP is required and in some circumstances, to senior management. The most common error in this area is underestimation. Because the former client is no longer "active", the firm may assume that risk is minimal. That assumption can be flawed. The duty of confidentiality is not transactional. It is permanent.

The professional question is simple – can the firm act in the new matter without drawing, even indirectly, on knowledge obtained in the former one? If the answer is not clear, then firm should proceed with caution and seriously consider whether they are able to continue to act.

CHAPTER FOUR

COMPLAINTS, NEGLIGENCE, AND REGULATORY PRESSURE

Complaints rarely arrive at convenient moments. They tend to surface when pressure is already high, such as during contentious litigation, when negotiations collapse, or in the final days before completion of a transaction. At precisely the point when the solicitor's focus should remain on the client's objectives, the firm suddenly finds itself confronting a different concern; protecting its own position.

At that moment two instincts collide. The first is the professional instinct that has guided the matter from the beginning which is the obvious, loyalty to the client, independence of judgment, and the obligation to continue acting in the client's best interests.

The second is more defensive. When criticism is directed at the firm, particularly in the form of a regulatory threat or negligence being alleged, the natural reaction is to protect the firm's reputation, its regulatory standing, sometimes its insurers, and also – yourself.

These pressures do not automatically create a conflict. The Code does not require a solicitor to withdraw simply because someone threatens to complain. Nor does a negligence allegation instantly make continued acting impossible. What the Code requires instead is something more measured, a calm detailed analysis, proper governance, and disciplined professional judgment. The real difficulty lies in maintaining that discipline while the pressure is mounting.

When the threat arrives

Most solicitors practising in contentious corporate work will recognise a familiar moment.

A firm acting for a company and its directors receives a letter from the solicitors for a disgruntled shareholder. The tone is aggressive. The firm is accused of lacking independence, of acting improperly, or of favouring one faction within the company. The letter ends with a warning that unless the firm ceases to act immediately, a report will be made to the SRA. Letters of this kind are rarely written to advance regulatory compliance. They are usually, tactical and are written to shift the dynamics of the dispute.

If the opposing firm can force the company's lawyers to withdraw, the balance of the litigation changes immediately. The client must instruct new advisers. The new advisers must learn the history of the dispute. Momentum is lost.

For that reason, regulatory threats sometimes appear in correspondence not because a breach has occurred, but because the threat itself creates pressure. Recognising that dynamic is important, however, it does not mean the threat should be dismissed.

The correct response is neither panic nor ignorance. It is analysis.

The first internal step

When criticism of this kind is received, the first step should not be drafting a response. It should be internal escalation. The firm's COLP should be notified promptly. Even where the allegation appears weak, early involvement of the firm's compliance function demonstrates governance discipline and ensures that the issue is assessed objectively rather than defensively.

The purpose of escalation is not to invite interference in the conduct of the matter. It is to ensure that the firm steps back and reassesses its position with fresh eyes.

At that point the firm should revisit the question it asked when the matter began – is the structure of representation still sound?

That means examining matters such as:

- whether the clients' interests remain aligned
- whether the company is giving instructions through a properly constituted board
- whether any new facts have emerged that might change the conflict analysis

Often the answer will be straightforward and that nothing material has changed, so the firm's original assessment remains valid. Where that is the case, the correct course is to record the analysis and continue acting.

Responding without escalation

Once the internal position has been reviewed, the response to the opposing firm should be measured and professional. Just because they have taken an aggressive tone, there is no need to rise to the bait. There is never any benefit in responding with equal aggression. Regulatory accusations tend to lose force when they are met with calm explanation rather than defensive rhetoric.

A clear response would explain why the firm considers its position consistent with the professional rules which is usually sufficient. The objective is not to persuade the other side, but to demonstrate that the firm has considered the issue carefully and remains confident in its analysis. In many cases, after a little more to-ing and fro-ing, the matter goes no further.

The regulatory threat has served its tactical purpose, and once it becomes clear that the firm will not withdraw simply because it has been asked to do so, the dispute returns to the substantive issues of the actual case.

When the pressure becomes internal

The more difficult situation arises when the pressure does not come from the other side but from within the client relationship itself. A client who is unhappy with the progress of a matter may suggest that the firm's earlier advice was wrong. A negotiation that collapses may lead to criticism of the legal strategy that was initially adopted. In extreme cases, a client may openly accuse the firm of negligence while the underlying matter is still ongoing.

At that point the solicitor faces a much more delicate problem. The issue is no longer merely external criticism. The solicitor must now consider whether defending the firm's own position risks affecting the advice being given to the client. If the solicitor begins to shape advice in order to protect the firm's earlier decisions, the independence of judgment required by the Code may be compromised.

This is the moment when careful professional reflection is required.

The subtle shift

One of the most difficult aspects of negligence allegations is that they rarely begin as formal claims. More often they appear as comments in conversation. A client may say; "*...if this goes wrong, I hope the firm* *will take responsibility...*", or "*...that isn't what we understood when we were advised last year...*". Comments of this kind do not necessarily amount to a formal allegation. But they signal that the relationship has changed. From that point onward, the solicitor must remain alert to a subtle but important risk: the possibility that the solicitor's personal interest in defending the firm may begin to influence the advice being given. When that happens, the issue moves beyond client dissatisfaction and begins to approach a genuine professional conflict.

The role of governance

Where concerns of this nature arise, the most important safeguard is transparency within the firm. The COLP, and often the firm's risk or professional indemnity team, should be informed. Early discussion allows the firm to consider whether the matter should continue with the existing team, whether additional supervision is required, or whether a different structure of representation may be necessary.

These conversations are rarely comfortable. Solicitors are trained to solve problems for clients, not to question their own position. But, the ability to recognise when independence may be at risk is an essential part of professional judgment.

Knowing when to step back

In many situations the correct decision will still be to continue acting. Clients can be critical without creating a genuine conflict, and withdrawing from every matter where criticism arises would make professional practice impossible. But, there are occasions when the solicitor must accept that the position has changed. If defending the firm's earlier advice becomes part of the ongoing dispute, or if the solicitor is required to advise the client about a course of action that may involve examining the firm's own conduct, the firm may no longer be able to provide the detached advice the client requires. At that point the responsible course may be to step aside.

Withdrawal in those circumstances is not an admission of fault. It is simply recognition that the client deserves advice that is entirely free from competing interests. It is important to remember, this is not personal.

The practical lesson

Complaints and negligence allegations are an inevitable part of professional life. The key is not to avoid them entirely, that is impossible, but to manage them without allowing them to distort professional judgment.

A well-run firm approaches these moments with structure:

- escalation to the COLP
- objective reassessment of the conflict position
- careful documentation of the reasoning
- calm communication with opponents and clients

In the end, the real test of professional integrity is not how a solicitor acts when matters are straightforward. It is how they act when criticism arrives.

CHAPTER FIVE

HIGH STREET CONFLICTS – SMALL COMMUNITIES, BIG RISKS

Conflicts in high street practice rarely announce themselves with complexity. In smaller firms and smaller communities, the solicitor is rarely advising strangers. They may have acted for the company for years, drafted its shareholders' agreement, perhaps a decade ago, advised the directors personally on refinancing their homes, and perhaps handled family matters for relatives. Relationships are layered, the files overlap, and instructions are often given informally. Trust is personal.

The risk in high street practice is not technical misunderstanding of the Code. It is the familiarity. For example, for years, alignment may appear effortless. Consider the earlier scenario of a company and its three directors for whom the firm has long acted. The firm drafted the constitutional documents, advised on governance, and handled routine disputes. There was no tension. Everyone's interests appeared to move in the same direction. Then litigation begins.

At first, the language remains collective. "…we just need to resolve this…", or "…it's a misunderstanding…". In smaller communities, those phrases carry emotional weight and pressure. The solicitor has known the individuals for years. There is a natural instinct to preserve cohesion. However, that does not substitute for analysis. The moment strain appears, the solicitor must consciously revisit the fundamentals, such as who is the client, is the company giving instructions through a properly constituted board, or are individual directors beginning to protect personal positions. You will need to ask – does the substantial common interest that justified joint representation still genuinely exist?

In high street practice, divergence is often incremental rather than dramatic. It rarely begins with open hostility. It may begin, as discussed earlier, with one director privately asking whether historic drafting exposed them to personal liability. That question, in a large commercial firm, may immediately trigger formal internal review. In a smaller firm, the temptation is to reassure informally. After all, the relationship is long standing. Yet that is precisely where discipline is required. Familiarity must not dilute structure. If advice to the company may differ from advice to an individual director, that distinction must be made explicit.

Founder led and family businesses make this distinction particularly difficult. In such environments, the company's identity often merges with that of its controllers. Board meetings may be informal, and instructions may be given collectively in a single conversation. While interests align, this works without difficulty. When drafting begins to affect personal wealth differently from corporate position, the distinction becomes critical. The solicitor must ensure that corporate instructions are properly authorised and not merely reflective of one faction's personal preferences.

Small communities also amplify the challenges of acting against former clients. A firm may have acted for Director A personally for years before the relationship ended amicably. The company, however, remains a long-standing client. When the company later seeks advice in proceedings against that former director, the issue is not divided loyalty between current clients. It is confidentiality. In a small practice, knowledge is rarely confined to documents. The firm may understand the former client's commercial instincts, financial pressures, appetite for litigation, or family dynamics. The passage of time does not necessarily offset that knowledge.

In larger firms, structural information barriers may provide reassurance. In a two- or three-partner high street practice, such barriers may be unrealistic. That does not mean acting is impossible. It means the analysis must be honest. The firm must identify precisely what information it holds, assess whether it remains relevant and confidential, and determine whether it can genuinely compartmentalise that knowledge. Escalation to the COLP is not disproportionate in these circumstances; it is good governance.

Complaint threats also feel different in small communities. A regulatory complaint in a local context can carry reputational consequences that extend beyond the immediate matter. Word travels quickly, and very often clients overlap socially and commercially. The instinct to withdraw in order to avoid community controversy can be strong. Yet the Code does not require withdrawal merely because criticism is voiced. The question remains the same as in larger practices; has independence been materially impaired, or is this external tactical pressure?

The transactional example explored earlier where a founder seeks enhanced personal protection late in an investment also plays out differently on the high street. The same solicitor may have acted for both founders personally for years. When incremental divergence appears, the relational dimension can make separation feel awkward or even disloyal. The founder may say, "…you've always acted for both of us….". That may be true historically. If enhanced exit protection reallocates risk in a way that benefits one at the potential expense of another represented client, the substantial common interest must be revisited. After all, past alignment does not guarantee present alignment.

Role creep is another subtle risk in smaller firms. The high street solicitor often becomes more than a technical adviser. They may be confidant, informal mediator, or long-standing business adviser. In director disputes, the solicitor may feel drawn into smoothing tensions while still formally acting for the company. That instinct is human and often commercially sensible. But mediation and representation are not the same role. The solicitor must remain clear, internally and externally, about which capacity they are acting in. Divided roles create divided loyalties.

The structural safeguards available to large commercial firms, such as separate teams, physical information barriers, formalised engagement segmentation are often not replicable in small practices. That does not leave high street firms exposed; it requires disciplined habits instead, such as:

- Clear engagement letters identifying precisely who the client is;
- Regular reassessment notes in multi-party matters;
- Formal confirmation of board authority before accepting instructions from companies in dispute;
- Early involvement of the COLP when long-standing clients begin to diverge; and
- Honest reflection on whether information barriers are realistic in a small team.

The greatest danger in high street conflict management is not ignorance of the rules. It is normalisation, such as "...we know the family...", or "...they wouldn't complain..."

The Code applies equally in a two-partner practice on a local high street and in an international firm. The underlying discipline remains unchanged: identify the client, test alignment, reassess when circumstances shift, and separate personal familiarity from professional duty.

Small communities do not create different rules. They create higher sensitivity to risk. And that risk lies not in complexity, but in closeness.

CHAPTER SIX

CONSENT IN PRACTICE

What informed consent really requires

Informed consent is often treated as an administrative step. A paragraph is inserted into an engagement letter, confirmation is signed, and the file is marked compliant. In practice, that approach is dangerously superficial. Informed consent is not achieved by disclosure alone. It requires understanding. And understanding cannot be assumed simply because a document has been signed.

The difficulty is that at the outset of most matters, clients are aligned. That alignment creates optimism. It also creates complacency.

The company and the directors

Take the familiar scenario, a firm acts for a company and its three directors in litigation. The directors have historically operated as a cohesive board. There is no internal hostility and the firm proposes to act under the substantial common interest exception. The engagement letter explains that the firm will act for both the company and the directors and that conflicts may arise. However, what does that mean in practical terms?

Informed consent in this scenario requires more than stating that divergence is possible. It requires explaining how divergence might realistically occur.

For example, the solicitor should explain:

- If the litigation strategy requires the company to take a position that exposes one director to greater personal criticism, the firm's primary duty in that context may be to the company;

- If one director provides information that is material to the company's position, the firm may not be able to keep that information confidential from the company;

- If directors begin to attribute fault to one another, the firm may be unable to continue acting for all of them.

These are uncomfortable conversations, but they need to happen. They can feel unnecessary at a stage when everyone appears united. Yet without, consent is theoretical rather than informed. It is protection, in case of a director who later says, "…I didn't realise you might have to step aside if things turned against me…", they have not given meaningful consent, even if they signed the letter.

In practice, the solicitor should document not just that consent was obtained, but what was explained. An attendance note recording that the directors were told explicitly that the firm could not favour individual interests if they diverged from the company's position may become critical if the relationship deteriorates later.

The investment transaction

Consider the investment scenario already explored. A firm acts for the company and its two founders. At heads of terms stage, the founders are aligned. They want the deal done. Valuation is agreed in principle, governance provisions are not yet contentious. It is tempting to present joint representation as efficient and straightforward. However, informed consent requires explaining where pressure is likely to arise.

The solicitor might say something along the lines of; "…as drafting progresses, issues such as leaver provisions, indemnities, and exit mechanics may affect each of you differently. If either of you seeks protection that reallocates risk in a way that disadvantages the other or the company, we may need to reconsider whether we can continue acting for all of you…"

This explanation does two things. It signals that divergence is foreseeable. And it sets expectations early. Without that conversation, a founder who later seeks enhanced exit protection may feel blindsided when told that separate advice is now required.

Informed consent must anticipate where friction is structurally likely to emerge, not merely state that friction is theoretically possible. This is key.

High street dynamics

In smaller practices, as mentioned, the difficulty is familiarity. A solicitor may have acted for the founders personally for years. The relationship is trusted and informal, and when explaining joint representation, the solicitor may feel awkward adopting a formal tone. The founders may respond with, "…we trust you, just get on with it..."

Trust does not eliminate the need for clarity. In high street settings, informed consent often fails because assumptions replace explanation. Everyone believes they understand the arrangement because the relationship is longstanding. Yet long-standing relationships can create greater risk if boundaries have never been articulated.

The solicitor should be explicit about role separation, such as saying "…if a disagreement arises between you, I will not be able to favour one of you over the other. At that point, one or both of you may need independent advice..." That sentence may feel uncomfortable in a friendly meeting room, but – necessary.

Consent under pressure

Another common weakness is timing. Consent obtained at the outset may be clear and thorough. But months later, circumstances may have shifted materially. In the litigation scenario, one director may begin privately questioning the firm's earlier drafting. In the investment scenario, one founder may begin negotiating protective provisions without openly acknowledging their strategic shift. At that stage, the original consent may no longer reflect reality. Informed consent is not static, it may require refreshing, and this does not mean reopening the entire engagement. It may involve a focused discussion – "...when we began acting jointly, you were aligned in your objectives. Recent developments suggest that your positions may diverge. We need to consider whether the original basis for joint representation still holds..."

Failing to revisit consent when circumstances evolve is one of the most common practical compliance failures.

Understanding the consequences

True informed consent requires that clients understand not only the risks but the consequences. For example:

- If divergence occurs, the firm may withdraw;
- Withdrawal may cause delay;
- Separate advice may increase cost;

- Information previously shared may not be retractable.

Clients must appreciate that joint representation carries practical implications. Without understanding the potential disruption, consent may be given casually and for all intent purposes, is academic.

What informed consent is not

It is not:

- A generic clause inserted into every engagement letter;
- A sentence stating that "conflicts may arise";
- A signature obtained without discussion;
- A one-off event at the beginning of a matter.

It is a continuing process of explanation and confirmation, grounded in the specific risks of the particular matter.

The professional discipline

In practice, informed consent requires three things beyond documentation:

- explaining foreseeable points of divergence in the actual matter;
- articulating the limits of confidentiality and loyalty in plain terms; and
- revisiting consent if the factual matrix changes.

The solicitor must be satisfied not merely that consent has been signed, but that it has been understood. The difference between procedural consent and informed consent is often invisible at the outset and only becomes visible only when there is divergence. At that moment, the quality of the original explanation determines whether the firm's position is defensible, both ethically and regulatorily.

CHAPTER SEVEN

PREVENTION, BETTER THAN CURE

Most conflict problems do not begin in the moment of crisis. They begin quietly, in the way the retainer was framed, in the way the client was identified, and in the assumptions left unchallenged at the outset of the relationship. By the time a conflict becomes visible, the structural groundwork has usually already been laid.

Lawyers are trained to analyse situations once they become difficult: when interests separate, when litigation begins, or when accusations are made.

But in practice, the most effective conflict management often happens long before any dispute arises.

The structure of an engagement; who the client is, what advice is being given, and how instructions are received determines how resilient the relationship will be if interests later diverge. When those foundations are unclear, conflict analysis becomes reactive and messy. When they are clear, the firm has options.

Conflict prevention therefore begins not with the conflict check itself, but with the way a matter is designed.

The basics

At the start of many corporate engagements, the question of who the client is appears obvious. The solicitor is instructed by a company, the instructions come from the directors. Everyone in the room understands that the advice is being given to the business.

Th most important question at the beginning of a matter is simple:

Who exactly is the client?

Answering that question clearly and documenting the answer, is the first line of defence against future conflict.

Engagement letters

Engagement letters are sometimes treated as administrative formalities. In reality, they are one of the most powerful conflict prevention tools available to a firm.

A well-constructed engagement letter does more than confirm fees and scope. It defines the legal relationship between the firm and the client.

Where a firm acts for a company in a matter involving directors or shareholders, the engagement letter should make that distinction explicit. It should explain that the firm acts for the company as a separate legal entity and that the directors or shareholders are not personal clients unless a separate engagement is agreed. This serves two purposes, first, it prevents misunderstandings about who is receiving legal advice. Second, it creates a clear reference point if interests later diverge.

Separate engagement letters for individuals where appropriate can be equally valuable. Rather than creating suspicion, they provide structural clarity. If a director later requires independent advice, the firm's existing documentation will already distinguish between corporate and personal representation.

Avoiding the trap of "acting for the Group"

Treating multiple companies as a single client can create serious difficulties later. When disputes arise between group entities, as they often do in restructuring, insolvency, or shareholder disputes, the firm may struggle to identify whose interests it is able to represent.

The approach is straightforward. Each new matter should identify which legal entity is the client. Even where ownership overlaps, the retainer should be specific. The firm should record which entity is instructing and through which authorised individual.

The risk of scope drift

Even where the client is clearly identified, the scope of advice can expand gradually. A transaction may begin with the firm advising the company. During the course of the work, a director asks about personal exposure under a warranty or a shareholder asks about tax consequences. Advice is offered conversationally, often in the spirit of helpfulness. However, over time, these interactions can create uncertainty about the scope of the firm's responsibilities.

Best thing to do, is to draft a short written confirmation along the lines of "…we are advising the Company on this transaction. We are not advising you personally on the personal or tax implications of these provisions. You may wish to obtain independent advice on those matters…"

Statements of this kind are not defensive. They are preventative.

Limited retainers

Limited retainers are sometimes viewed with caution. Clients may assume they reflect a lack of commitment or an attempt to restrict responsibility.

In reality, they are often the most practical way to manage complex engagements involving multiple stakeholders.

For example, in an investment transaction a firm may act for the company in negotiating the deal while making clear that it does not advise the founders personally on tax planning or personal exit arrangements. In a corporate dispute, the firm may represent the company alone while explaining that individual directors should obtain separate representation if personal liability becomes relevant.

Limited retainers do not eliminate conflict risk entirely, but they significantly reduce the situations in which the firm becomes structurally entangled in competing personal interests.

Internal systems that support prevention

Conflict prevention is not achieved by engagement letters alone. It also depends on internal discipline within the firm.

Many well-run firms support this discipline through practical systems.

File notes are an often underestimated safeguard. When advice is given in circumstances where client roles may be ambiguous, a short contemporaneous note can clarify the context. Recording who was present, who requested advice, and on whose behalf it was given can be invaluable later.

Internal escalation is another important safeguard. Where fee earners encounter situations that may expand the scope of representation, for example advising directors personally in a corporate matter, early discussion with the firm's COLP or risk team can help ensure that the engagement structure remains appropriate.

Training also plays an important role. Junior lawyers and trainees often participate in meetings where directors and shareholders ask questions informally. Without training, they may assume that answering those questions forms part of the firm's retainer. Firms that regularly train their teams on client identification and scope management reduce the risk of these misunderstandings.

Finally, **internal policies** on engagement letters and client identification provide consistency. Standard templates that clearly distinguish between corporate and personal representation help ensure that good practice becomes routine rather than discretionary.

Planning the exit

Another aspect of engagement design that receives little attention is the question of disengagement. If interests later diverge, how will the firm withdraw?

Raising this possibility at the outset may feel uncomfortable, but it is often sensible. Explaining that the firm may need to cease acting for one or all parties if interests diverge prepares clients for the possibility and avoids surprise later.

Equally important is explaining that information already shared within a joint representation cannot easily be separated afterwards. Once confidential information has been exchanged between aligned clients, it may limit the firm's ability to continue acting for either party if a dispute emerges.

These conversations are easier at the beginning of a matter than during a dispute.

In smaller firms, structural precision can feel unnecessary. Relationships with clients may extend over many years and form distinctions between the company and the individuals behind it can feel artificial. Yet these circumstances often increase conflict risk rather than reduce it.

Where relationships are close, assumptions about who the firm represents may remain unexamined for long periods. The closer the relationship, the more valuable clarity becomes.

Most conflict crises do not arise because lawyers misunderstand the rules, they arise because the structure of representation was never clearly defined. The firms that manage conflict well are usually the firms that invest time in designing their engagements carefully before the work begins.

CHAPTER EIGHT

CONFLICT MANAGEMENT AS PROFESSIONAL JUDGMENT

Conflicts of interest are often discussed as though they were mechanical rules. The Code sets out the framework, the paragraphs are clear, and the categories are defined. In theory, the answer should simply follow from applying the rule to the facts.

In practice, we know it is rarely that straightforward.

Conflicts are not usually obvious at the moment they first appear. They develop gradually, often within relationships that have existed for years and in matters that began with genuine alignment between clients. What appears manageable at one stage may become unsustainable later as facts evolve and interests shift. For that reason, conflict management is not simply a technical exercise. It is an exercise in professional judgment.

The Code provides the structure. It defines the boundaries that solicitors must operate within and establishes when acting is prohibited and when it may be permitted with appropriate safeguards. But the Code does not remove the need for judgment. It expects solicitors to assess the factual reality of the situation in front of them and to recognise when circumstances have changed. That judgment must be exercised continuously. A conflict assessment made at the outset of a matter cannot remain static if the facts evolve. Alignment between clients may weaken, litigation may develop in unexpected ways, or commercial negotiations may begin to allocate risk differently between parties who were previously united in purpose.

Good firms recognise that these moments are inevitable. Rather than relying on instinct alone, they create structures that support careful decision making. They document their reasoning, involve the COLP where appropriate, and reassess their position when the circumstances of a matter shift.

Documentation and governance are sometimes misunderstood as defensive measures. In reality they serve a more important purpose. They ensure that decisions are made deliberately rather than reactively, and that the firm can demonstrate that its judgment was grounded in the facts and the regulatory framework at the time.

Equally important is recognising that conflict management is not about avoiding difficult decisions. There will be occasions when a firm must withdraw from a matter because the alignment that once justified acting no longer exists. When that point is reached, stepping aside is not a failure of judgment. It is evidence that professional obligations are being taken seriously.

The purpose of this book has not been to suggest that conflicts can always be avoided, they cannot. Complex commercial relationships, long-standing client connections, and evolving disputes make them an inevitable part of legal practice.

What solicitors can do is approach those situations with clarity and discipline; identifying the client, testing alignment carefully, documenting decisions, and revisiting those decisions when circumstances change. Ultimately, conflict management is not about rigid adherence to rules in isolation. It is about applying those rules thoughtfully within the realities of professional practice.

The Code sets the framework. Professional judgment brings it to life.

PRACTICAL TOOLS FOR MANAGING CONFLICTS

APPENDIX A

CONFLICT DECISION FLOWCHART – SHOULD THE FIRM CONTINUE ACTING?

This decision guide is not a substitute for professional judgment. It is designed to assist solicitors in identifying the key questions that should be considered when a potential conflict arises.

<u>Step 1 – Identify the client</u>

Before assessing any conflict, confirm:

- Who is the client in this matter?
- Is the firm acting for:
  - a company?
  - individual directors or shareholders?
  - multiple parties?

Key question:

Is the client clearly identified in the engagement letter?

If the answer is unclear, the firm should clarify the client relationship before continuing.

Step 2 – Are there multiple clients in the matter?

Ask:

- Is the firm acting for more than one party in this matter?
- For example:
    - a company and its directors
    - multiple shareholders
    - companies entering into a joint venture
    - founders in an investment transaction

If the firm acts for only one client, proceed to Step 6 (former client and confidentiality considerations).

If there are multiple clients, continue to Step 3.

Step 3 – Is there an own interest conflict?

Consider whether the solicitor or firm has a personal interest in the matter.

Examples include:

- a financial interest in the outcome
- advising on or defending the firm's own conduct
- a personal relationship that may impair independence

- circumstances where the firm's commercial interest could influence advice

Key question is would the solicitor's personal interests risk conflicting with the client's best interests?

If the answer is yes, this may be an own interest conflict.

The firm must not act. This type of conflict cannot be cured by consent or safeguards.

If no personal conflict exists, continue to Step 4.

Step 4 – Is there a conflict between clients?

Consider whether the firm owes duties to multiple clients whose interests conflict or may conflict.

Ask:

- Do the clients have different objectives in the matter?
- Could acting for one client disadvantage another?
- Is there a significant risk that their interests may diverge as the matter develops?

If the answer is yes, proceed to Step 5.

Step 5 – Can the firm rely on an exception?

Where a client conflict exists, the firm may only act if one of the following applies.

1) Substantially Common Interest

Ask:

- Do the clients share a clear common objective?
- Are they aligned not only in outcome but in strategy?
- Is the alignment genuine rather than temporary convenience?

Example:

Company and directors jointly defending litigation.

2) Competing for the same objective

Example – two parties bidding for the same asset in a structured process.

If neither exception applies, the firm should not act for both clients.

If an exception applies, proceed to Step 6.

Step 6 – Can the conditions be satisfied?

Even where an exception applies, three further conditions must be met.

The firm must ensure:

Informed consent – All affected clients must understand the risks and confirm consent in writing.

Confidentiality safeguards – Where necessary, the firm must protect confidential information through appropriate safeguards.

Reasonableness – The firm must be satisfied that it is reasonable to act for all clients.

Key question is can the firm realistically maintain loyalty and confidentiality to each client?

If not, the firm should not continue acting.

Step 7 – Consider former client confidentiality

Even if the firm acts for only one current client, consider:

- Has the firm previously acted for another party involved in the matter?
- Does the firm hold confidential information that could be relevant?

Ask:

- Could the firm's knowledge create an unfair advantage?
- Could advice be influenced by confidential information obtained previously?

If the answer is yes, the firm should carefully consider whether acting is appropriate.

Escalation to the COLP may be required.

Step 8 – Document the assessment

If the firm decides it can continue acting, the reasoning should be recorded.

A file note should include:

- the nature of the potential conflict
- the basis on which acting is considered permissible
- confirmation of informed consent
- any safeguards implemented
- when the position will next be reviewed

Documentation ensures that the decision is grounded in analysis rather than assumption.

Step 9 – Monitor the situation

Conflict assessment is not a one-time exercise.

Throughout the matter, ask:

- Have the clients' interests changed?
- Are new facts emerging that affect alignment?
- Has any client begun pursuing a position adverse to another?

If circumstances change, the conflict analysis should be revisited.

Practical reminder

Conflicts often become visible only gradually.

The key safeguards are:

- clear identification of the client
- careful documentation of decisions
- early escalation where uncertainty exists
- regular reassessment as the matter develops

When used consistently, these steps help ensure that conflict decisions remain structured, defensible and aligned with professional obligations.

APPENDIX B

PRACTICAL QUESTIONS SOLICITORS SHOULD ASK WHEN CONFLICTS ARISE

<u>Questions About client identity</u>

- Who is the client in this matter?
- Is the client the company or the individuals behind it?
- Are instructions being given through the correct governance structure?

<u>Questions about alignment</u>

- Do the clients genuinely share the same objective?
- Are they aligned on strategy, not just outcome?
- Could the advice required for one client disadvantage another?

<u>Questions about confidential information</u>

- Does the firm hold confidential information from another client or former client?
- Could that information be relevant to this matter?

- Could acting create an unfair advantage?

Questions about governance

- Has the conflict assessment been documented?
- Has the COLP been consulted where appropriate?
- Have clients been properly informed about risks?

Questions about practical reality

- If the clients begin to disagree, could the firm realistically continue acting?
- Would the firm be forced to withdraw from everyone?

If the answer is yes, reconsider acting at the outset.

APPENDIX C

TEMPLATE DOCUMENTS

Template 1 – Conflict file note

Matter: [Insert matter name]
Client(s): [Insert client names]
Date: [Insert date]
Prepared by: [Insert name]

1. Nature of the Matter

Brief description of the instruction:

[The firm has been instructed by ABC Ltd in relation to shareholder litigation involving a former shareholder. The firm has previously acted for certain directors of the company personally]

2. Clients represented in this Matter

List the clients for whom the firm proposes to act.

Example:

- ABC Ltd (company)
- Director A (personal capacity)
- Director B (personal capacity)

3. Potential conflict identified

Describe the potential conflict or risk.

[The firm acts for both the company and individual directors. There is a risk that interests could diverge if the litigation requires the company to adopt a position adverse to a director]

4. Conflict category

Assess whether the issue involves:

- an own interest conflict (Paragraph 6.1), or
- a client conflict (Paragraph 6.2).

Example:

[No personal interest conflict identified. Potential client conflict exists between the company and the directors]

5. Exception relied upon

If applicable, identify the exception relied upon.

Example:

[Substantially common interest. The company and directors are currently aligned in defending the claim]

6. Informed consent

Confirm how consent has been obtained.

Example:

[Written informed consent obtained from all clients via engagement letter dated [insert date]]

7. Safeguards

Describe any safeguards implemented.

Examples:

- separate files maintained
- clear distinction between advice to company and individuals
- regular review of alignment

8. Reasonableness assessment

Explain why it is reasonable for the firm to act.

Example:

[The clients' objectives remain aligned and no adverse positions have emerged]

9. Review date

Conflict assessment to be reviewed on:

[Insert date]

Template 2 – Reassessment during the Matter

Matter: [Insert matter name]

Date: [Insert date]

Reason for Reassessment

Example:

[Director A has requested advice regarding potential personal liability arising from earlier board decisions]

Updated Analysis

Explain whether alignment has changed.

Example:

[The request may indicate a divergence between the director's personal interests and the company's position]

Action taken

Examples:

- advice provided that personal legal advice may be required
- matter escalated to COLP
- joint representation reviewed

Conclusion

Example:

[At present, alignment remains sufficient to justify continued acting. Position to be monitored]

Template 3 – Withdrawal Decision

Matter: [Insert matter name]

Date: [Insert date]

Reason for Withdrawal

Example:

[Clients' interests have diverged to the extent that the firm can no longer act for both parties without compromising duties of loyalty and confidentiality]

Steps taken

Examples:

- clients informed of the conflict
- recommendation that independent legal advice be obtained
- file transfer arrangements discussed

Record of decision

Example:

[Following internal review and consultation with the COLP, the firm concluded that continued acting would no longer be reasonable under Paragraph 6.2]

APPENDIX D

WARNING SIGNS THAT ALIGNMENT MAY BE BREAKING DOWN

The following warning signs are commonly observed in practice.

<u>Requests for private conversations</u>

One of the earliest signals of divergence is when a client asks to speak to the solicitor privately about issues affecting the matter.

Examples include:

- a director asking to speak "off the record"
- a shareholder requesting confidential advice about how a clause affects them personally
- a founder asking how to "protect themselves" if things go wrong

Private conversations of this nature are not inherently improper. However, they may indicate that the individual is beginning to view their interests separately from the shared objective that justified joint representation.

If information disclosed privately could affect the interests of other represented clients, the solicitor must carefully consider whether confidentiality can realistically be maintained.

Attempts to modify drafting for personal advantage

In transactional matters, divergence often appears first in drafting.

Examples include:

- requests to amend indemnities or warranties that shift risk between represented clients
- adjustments to exit provisions benefiting one founder over another
- modifications to voting rights or governance provisions favouring one faction

These requests are often framed as minor drafting changes, but their commercial effect may be significant. A solicitor should consider whether advising on such changes would require advancing one client's interests at the expense of another.

Instructions that conflict with board decisions

In corporate matters, instructions should normally be given through the company's proper governance structure.

Warning signs may include:

- individual directors attempting to override board decisions
- requests for advice that contradict the company's stated position
- instructions given informally rather than through authorised governance channels

If instructions appear to reflect the interests of individuals rather than the company as a separate legal entity, the solicitor should reassess whether they are acting for the company or effectively for a particular faction.

Attribution of blame between clients

Conflicts often crystallise when clients begin attributing responsibility to one another.

Examples include:

- one director suggesting another caused the dispute
- shareholders questioning earlier decisions made by fellow shareholders
- clients suggesting that another party's actions have exposed them to liability

Once blame begins to circulate among represented clients, the solicitor may be placed in a position where advising one client requires criticising another.

At that stage, the substantial common interest that previously justified acting may no longer exist.

Requests for advice on personal liability

Another common signal arises when individual clients seek advice about personal risk.

Examples include:

- directors asking about exposure under warranties
- shareholders asking whether they could face personal claims
- founders seeking advice about removal or exit scenarios

While these questions are often commercially reasonable, they may signal that personal interests are beginning to diverge from collective objectives.

If the advice required would differ between clients, the firm must consider whether it can continue acting for all of them.

Settlement discussions that reveal diverging objectives

Settlement discussions can also reveal hidden divergence.

Examples include:

- one client seeking early settlement while others wish to continue litigation
- different views about acceptable commercial outcomes
- proposals that benefit one party but disadvantage another represented client

If settlement strategy requires the solicitor to advocate different positions for different clients, joint representation may no longer be sustainable.

Increasingly defensive behaviour by clients

Changes in tone can also indicate emerging divergence.

Examples include:

- clients becoming reluctant to share information
- requests that discussions remain confidential from other clients
- reluctance to attend joint meetings

These behavioural shifts may reflect a growing awareness that interests are no longer fully aligned.

Requests to limit information sharing

A particularly important warning sign occurs when a client asks the solicitor not to share certain information with another represented client.

For example:

- "Don't tell the others I said this."
- "This is just between us."

In joint representations, the solicitor must be clear about the limits of confidentiality between clients.

If information cannot be shared without harming another client's interests, the firm may need to reconsider whether it can continue acting.

External pressure from opposing parties

Opposing parties may attempt to exploit potential conflicts by raising regulatory concerns.

Examples include:

- allegations that the firm lacks independence
- threats to report the firm to the SRA
- suggestions that the firm is favouring one client

These allegations do not automatically create a conflict. However, they may highlight issues that require careful internal reassessment.

The "something feels wrong" moment

Experienced solicitors often recognise divergence before it is formally articulated.

The instinct that "something no longer feels aligned" should not be ignored.

When that feeling arises, the appropriate response is to pause and reassess the conflict position rather than assume the issue will resolve itself.

Practical approach

When warning signs appear, firms should consider:

- documenting the concern

- reassessing the conflict analysis
- discussing the issue internally
- escalating to the COLP where appropriate

Early reassessment can often prevent a manageable risk from becoming a disqualifying conflict.

APPENDIX E

SAMPLE ENGAGEMENT LETTER CLAUSES

Acting for a Company only clause

The firm acts for the Company only. We do not act for its directors, shareholders or employees personally unless expressly agreed in writing. Where advice is given in meetings attended by directors or shareholders, that advice is provided to the Company as a separate legal entity.

Individuals should obtain independent advice if personal interests arise.

Joint representation clause

If circumstances arise where the interests of the parties diverge, the firm may be required to cease acting for one or all parties.

Information disclosed by one client may not be treated as confidential as between the clients in matters where we act jointly.

APPENDIX F

CHECKLIST FOR FIRMS

Confirm:

- ☐ client identity documented
- ☐ engagement letter clear
- ☐ consent obtained (if needed)
- ☐ safeguards considered
- ☐ file note created
- ☐ COLP notified if complex
- ☐ review date diarised

MORE BOOKS BY LAW BRIEF PUBLISHING

A selection of our other titles available now:-

'A Practical Guide to Probation Breaches and Other Applications' by Mark Thomas
'A Practical Guide to Remarriage and Divorce' by Cordelia Williams & Claire Howard
'A Practical Guide to Privacy, Transparency, Reporting Restrictions and Closed Proceedings in the Court of Protection' by Laura Mannering
'Beaumont on Barristers – A Guide to Defending Disciplinary Proceedings (Second Edition)' by Marc Beaumont
'A Practical Guide to Payments for Environmental Services' by Ben Sharples
'A Practical Guide to the Law of Pregnancy and Maternity at Work' by Rebecca Thomas
'A Practical Guide to Redundancy – Second Edition' by Philip Hyland & Collette Moore
'A Practical Guide to International Issues for Scottish Family Lawyers' by Susie Mountain, Donna McKay, Ken MacDonald
'A Practical Guide to the Law on Deprivation of Liberty' by Ben Troke
'A Practical Guide to Rights over Airspace and Subsoil – Second Edition' by Daniel Gatty
'A Practical Guide to the Law in Relation to Inquests' by Ramya Nagesh
'A Practical Guide to the Construction and Rectification of Wills and Trust Instruments (Second Edition)' by Edward Hewitt
'A Practical Guide to Data Protection in Social Housing' by Clare Paterson
'A Practical Guide to Spousal Maintenance – Second Edition' by Liz Cowell
'A Practical Guide to International Parental Child Abduction Law (England and Wales)' by Dr Onyója Momoh
'A Practical Guide to Deprivation of British Citizenship' by Sean Ell
'A Practical Guide to Commercial Property Service Charges' by Rachel Garton
'A Practical Guide to Clinical Negligence – Third Edition' by Geoffrey Simpson-Scott (Geoff)
'A Practical Guide to the Rights of Grandparents in Children Proceedings – Second Edition' by Stuart Barlow

‘Stephens on Contractual Indemnities’ by Richard Stephens

‘A Practical Guide to the EU Succession Regulation’ by Richard Frimston

‘A Practical Guide to Solicitor and Client Costs – Second Edition’ by Robin Dunne

‘Constructive Dismissal – Practice Pointers and Principles’ by Benjimin Burgher

‘A Practical Guide to Religion and Belief Discrimination Claims in the Workplace’ by Kashif Ali

‘A Practical Guide to the Law of Medical Treatment Decisions’ by Ben Troke

‘Fundamental Dishonesty and QOCS in Personal Injury Proceedings: Law and Practice’ by Jake Rowley

‘A Practical Guide to the Law in Relation to School Exclusions’ by Charlotte Hadfield & Alice de Coverley

‘A Practical Guide to Divorce for the Silver Separators’ by Karin Walker

‘The Right to be Forgotten – The Law and Practical Issues’ by Melissa Stock

‘A Practical Guide to Planning Law and Rights of Way in National Parks, the Broads and AONBs’ by James Maurici QC, James Neill et al

‘A Practical Guide to Election Law’ by Tom Tabori

‘A Practical Guide to the Law in Relation to Surrogacy’ by Andrew Powell

‘A Practical Guide to Claims Arising from Fatal Accidents – Second Edition’ by James Patience

‘A Practical Guide to Asbestos Claims’ by Jonathan Owen & Gareth McAloon

‘A Practical Guide to Stamp Duty Land Tax in England and Northern Ireland’ by Suzanne O’Hara

‘A Practical Guide to the Law of Farming Partnerships’ by Philip Whitcomb

‘A Practical Guide to the Law of Unlawful Eviction and Harassment – Second Edition’ by Stephanie Lovegrove

‘A Practical Guide to Costs in Personal Injury Claims – Second Edition’ by Matthew Hoe

‘A Practical Guide to the General Data Protection Regulation (GDPR) – Second Edition’ by Keith Markham

‘A Practical Guide to Working with Litigants in Person and McKenzie Friends in Family Cases’ by Stuart Barlow

‘Protecting Unregistered Brands: A Practical Guide to the Law of Passing Off’ by Lorna Brazell

‘A Practical Guide to Secondary Liability and Joint Enterprise Post-Jogee’ by Joanne Cecil & James Mehigan

'A Practical Guide to the Pre-Action RTA Claims Protocol for Personal Injury Lawyers' by Antonia Ford

'A Practical Guide to Neighbour Disputes and the Law' by Alexander Walsh

'A Practical Guide to Coercive Control for Legal Practitioners and Victims' by Rachel Horman

'A Practical Guide to the Law of Driverless Cars – Second Edition'

by Alex Glassbrook, Emma Northey & Scarlett Milligan

'A Practical Guide to TOLATA Claims' by Greg Williams

'A Practical Guide to Elderly Law – Second Edition' by Justin Patten

'A Practical Guide to Responding to Housing Disrepair and Unfitness Claims' by Iain Wightwick

'A Practical Guide to the Law of Bullying and Harassment in the Workplace' by Philip Hyland

'How to Be a Freelance Solicitor: A Practical Guide to the SRA-Regulated Freelance Solicitor Model' by Paul Bennett

'A Practical Guide to Prison Injury Claims' by Malcolm Johnson

'A Practical Guide to Advising Clients at the Police Station' by Colin Stephen McKeown-Beaumont

'A Practical Guide to Antisocial Behaviour Injunctions – Second Edition' by Iain Wightwick

'Practical Mediation: A Guide for Mediators, Advocates, Advisers, Lawyers, and Students in Civil, Commercial, Business, Property, Workplace, and Employment Cases' by Jonathan Dingle with John Sephton

'The Mini-Pupillage Workbook' by David Boyle

'A Practical Guide to Crofting Law' by Brian Inkster

'A Practical Guide to the Law of Domain Names and Cybersquatting' by Andrew Clemson

'A Practical Guide to the Law of Gender Pay Gap Reporting' by Harini Iyengar

'NHS Whistleblowing and the Law' by Joseph England

'Employment Law and the Gig Economy' by Nigel Mackay & Annie Powell

'A Practical Guide to Noise Induced Hearing Loss (NIHL) Claims' by Andrew Mckie, Ian Skeate, Gareth McAloon

'An Introduction to Beauty Negligence Claims – A Practical Guide for the Personal Injury Practitioner' by Greg Almond

'Intercompany Agreements for Transfer Pricing Compliance' by Paul Sutton

'Zen and the Art of Mediation' by Martin Plowman

'A Practical Guide to Adoption for Family Lawyers' by Graham Pegg

www.ingramcontent.com/pod-product-compliance
Lightning Source LLC
LaVergne TN
LVHW022303200926
848481LV00004B/1198
9781918241310